Portage Public Library
2665 Irving Street
Portage, IN 46368

EDMONIA
LEWIS

Internationally Renowned Sculptor

Celebrating

BLACK ARTISTS

EDMONIA
LEWIS

Internationally Renowned Sculptor

Enslow Publishing
101 W. 23rd Street
Suite 240
New York, NY 10011
USA
enslow.com

CHARLOTTE ETINDE-CROMPTON AND
SAMUEL WILLARD CROMPTON

Published in 2020 by Enslow Publishing, LLC
101 W. 23rd Street, Suite 240, New York, NY 10011

Library of Congress Cataloging-in-Publication Data

Names: Etinde-Crompton, Charlotte, author. | Crompton, Samuel Willard, author.
Title: Edmonia Lewis : internationally renowned sculptor / Charlotte Etinde-Crompton and Samuel Willard Crompton.
Description: New York : Enslow Publishing, 2020. | Series: Celebrating black artists | Includes bibliographical references and index. | Audience: Grades 7-12.
Identifiers: LCCN 2019004360| ISBN 9781978514713 (library bound) | ISBN 9781978514706 (pbk.)
Subjects: LCSH: Lewis, Edmonia—Juvenile literature. | African American sculptors—Biography—Juvenile literature.
Classification: LCC NB237.L487 E85 2020 | DDC 730.92 [B] —dc23
LC record available at https://lccn.loc.gov/2019004360

Printed in China

To Our Readers: We have done our best to make sure all website addresses in this book were active and appropriate when we went to press. However, the author and the publisher have no control over and assume no liability for the material available on those websites or on any websites they may link to. Any comments or suggestions can be sent by email to customerservice@enslow.com.

Contents

A Connection with Frederick Douglass

In the nineteenth century, Mary Edmonia Lewis achieved a feat that few would have thought possible: she became a professional sculptor. Of black and Native American ancestry, Lewis excelled as an artist despite the fierce discrimination she faced as a woman of color. Both her determination and passion for her craft saw her through challenges that would have led others to give up on their dreams. But Lewis did everything she could to succeed, even moving from the United States to Italy to make a living. The artist also made sculptures she knew would be in high demand and befriended people with the connections to advance her career.

Befriending the Douglasses

The abolitionists were one group of people Lewis turned to for career help. She made sculptures of these activists, who fought to end slavery, in hopes that they would spread the word about her work or buy it themselves—and they did. Among her abolitionist friends was Frederick Douglass, an African American who'd escaped slavery to become one

Edmonia Lewis was the first sculptor of African American and Native American origin to become world famous. Both Europeans and Americans admired her work.

of the institution's most famous opponents. Douglass had personally met with President Abraham Lincoln to discuss ending slavery and the treatment of black soldiers during the Civil War.

The abolitionist and his second wife, Helen Pitts Douglass, got to know Edmonia Lewis when they visited Rome in 1887. The Eternal City was not as grand as it once was, as the wars to unify Italy in the previous decades

The Grand Tour

From the late seventeenth century through the eighteenth century, traveling across western Europe became a tradition for privileged young men from the United States and Europe alike.[1] The rite of passage was called the Grand Tour and could last for a few months or up to five years. It marked a time for the travelers to learn about philosophers, artists, and literary figures.

In Rome, they would tour sites such as the Coliseum and St. Peter's tomb. But by the 1800s, the Grand Tour began to fall out of fashion. Still, visits to Europe remained a symbol of social status, and the expansion of a railway across the continent made travel there even more convenient—for men and women alike.

After Edmonia Lewis traveled to Europe, she stayed there for good. As an African American sculptor, she was not just unusual but may have been the only such artist on the continent.

had ravaged Rome. But the Douglasses were mostly interested in the history of the city, especially its art. This interest led the couple to spend time with Edmonia Lewis, the city's only African American sculptor.

When the Douglasses arrived in Rome, Lewis had lived there for about twenty years. She spoke Italian fluently and knew many, if not most, of the city's artistic and cultural treasures. She welcomed the Douglasses into her art studio and showed them around, treating them much differently from how they'd been received in the United States. That's because Helen Pitts Douglass was a white woman roughly twenty years her husband's junior, and both whites and blacks, including Douglass's children, had objected to the marriage. They couldn't understand why Douglass had married outside the African American community.

Laws against miscegenation, or mixing of the races, were on the books of several states, and society largely viewed a black person marrying a white person as unnatural, if not immoral.

In this undated photo, the structure called the Castel Sant'Angelo (right) and the bridge called the Ponte Sant'Angelo stand over the Tiber River. Saint Peter's Basilica appears in the background.

Suffragist and abolitionist Helen Pitts Douglass sits with her famous husband Frederick Douglass near Niagara Falls. Their interracial marriage was met with wide disapproval.

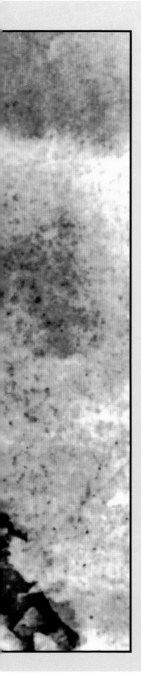

Helen Pitts Douglass

Helen Pitts Douglass was born in 1838 in Honeoye, New York. She was a suffragist, or an an activist who worked for women's right to vote, and an abolitionist.

In 1859, Pitts graduated from Mount Holyoke Female Seminary and then taught at Virginia's Hampton Institute, which served freedmen after the Civil War. She moved to Washington, DC, working for women's rights journal *The Alpha* in 1880. The next year, she met Frederick Douglass, Washington's recorder of deeds and her next-door neighbor. Douglass ended up hiring Pitts as a clerk in the deeds office.

After Douglass's first wife, Anne Murray Douglass, died in 1882, his relationship with Pitts turned romantic. They wed on January 24, 1884, prompting the *New York Times* to note that Pitts was white and young enough to be Douglass' daughter.[2]

Still, the couple toured Europe together and later lived in Haiti when Frederick was appointed a US minister there. When he died in 1895, Helen worked to establish a memorial for him, now the Frederick Douglass National Historic Site.

Helen Pitts Douglass died in 1903.

Douglass seldom addressed the criticism of his marriage, telling those bold enough to raise the issue with him to mind their own business. And to show the world how much he valued his new wife, a feminist and abolitionist, Douglass announced that they would tour the historic sites of western Europe together.

"We go together as you and I do," Helen Pitts Douglass wrote her sister, "looking slowly at what we want to see, and passing by what we do not want to see—and generally wanting to see the same things."[3]

Edmonia Lewis, who was of mixed race ancestry herself, did not judge Frederick and Helen Douglass for becoming husband and wife. It helped that Frederick Douglass's trip to Italy wasn't the first time she'd met the abolitionist. Their first encounter had taken place several years earlier, and Douglass, evidently, had been impressed enough with Lewis to renew their acquaintance when he arrived in Italy.

He enjoyed his time with the sculptor and wrote that she'd been in Italy for so long that she no longer spoke English very well. But Lewis had not spent her early childhood speaking English, as she had learned Native American dialects, such as Ojibwe, from her family first.[4] Any language barrier between the Douglasses and Lewis did not significantly interfere with their friendship. Douglass found her outgoing, cheerful, and happy with her life in Rome.

But it was Helen Pitts Douglass who really warmed to Lewis. The two spent many hours in each other's company, traveling to art museums together in Rome and Naples. Struggling with the criticism of her interracial marriage,

Helen felt fortunate to have found Lewis. We do not know exactly why the two formed a connection, but Lewis might have explained that her own racial and ethnic story was not as simple as it first appeared. Culturally Ojibwe (or Chippewa) but African American in appearance, Lewis had experienced bias from all corners of society.

Race, Ethnicity, and Religion

In the nineteenth century, both Native Americans and African Americans routinely had their humanity questioned. Both groups were viewed as inferior to whites, an idea that was used to deprive them of land rights, human rights, and more. But this period also saw the Civil War and the passing of the Constitution's Thirteenth, Fourteenth, and Fifteenth Amendments, all of which made African Americans full citizens on paper. (Native Americans weren't granted citizenship until 1924.) Despite the constitutional rights they'd been granted, black Americans were treated as second-class citizens in the 1800s and continued to be thought of as less capable than whites. Many whites thought blacks were suitable for physical labor but not for jobs that required intellect and talent, such as running a business, writing literature, or creating art.

Frederick Douglass had proven that enslaved blacks could excel in life if given the opportunity. He had become a journalist, speaker, and activist after escaping slavery. But white Americans who refused to believe that blacks could be their equals wrote Douglass off as an exception to the rule. This makes the achievements of Edmonia Lewis even more important. Since she was a woman of color, few thought she could do anything other than become a wife, mother, or housekeeper.

Through her smarts and willpower, Lewis defied expectations by becoming a world-famous artist. This achievement took her time, of course, and she faced numerous obstacles along the way. But her eventual success challenged longstanding stereotypes about African Americans, Native Americans, and women. It announced to the world that women of color were every bit as capable as their white counterparts.

Edmonia's Early Years

$\mathbf{A}$s if for sport, Mary Edmonia Lewis often altered the details of her life and played with its chronology. This has made it difficult for historians and biographers to know just how her life unfolded. Even her birthdate is unknown, but scholars believe she was born sometime around July 4, 1844, in Greenbush, New York. Today, Greenbush is the city of Rensselaer, located on the eastern side of the Hudson River, right across from Albany.[1]

In 1844, the Albany area was in the middle of a commercial and industrial boom that would last for decades. Many fortunes were made, especially in the dry-goods industry. Albany was already an important stop along the Erie Canal transport system, and it was about to become a center for railroad lines as well. As Albany embraced industrialization, however, some of its residents led lives that clashed with the region's rapid growth. These residents included the Lewis family.

Edmonia Lewis's Girlhood

Edmonia Lewis's maternal grandfather was said to be an African American who had escaped from slavery. Her

STATE STREET AND CAPITOL, ALBANY, NEW YORK.

This is an 1850 view of the state capitol building along State Street in Albany, New York. Edmonia Lewis grew up in this area.

maternal grandmother, on the other hand, belonged to the Chippewa, or Ojibwe, people. This made her mother a mixture of black and Native American, and both groups would have a major impact on Edmonia's life.

While her mother, a weaver and craftswoman, was biracial, Edmonia's father was an Afro-Haitian man who'd moved to New York and worked as a gentleman's servant. It's unclear how her parents met, but at some point, they moved to Greenbush, and Edmonia was born shortly afterward.[2]

The baby girl had a half-brother named Samuel Lewis, who was nine years her senior; he was born in Haiti to her father's first wife. Despite their age difference, the two became best friends and playmates. But when Edmonia was a small girl, both of her parents died. As a result, she and her brother moved in with her mother's Chippewa sisters in the Buffalo region near Niagara Falls. She would later describe this part of her life as heavenly. She loved wandering in the woods with her brother, embroidering moccasins with her aunts, and selling souvenirs to tourists.

"She passed the first twelve years of her life in the wilds, fishing, swimming, hunting, and making moccasins," according to an early biographer.[3] It's doubtful that Edmonia had any formal schooling during this period, but she always recalled this part of her childhood fondly. "I often longed to return to the wilds, but my love of sculpture forbade it,"[4] she said as an adult. Edmonia may have very well loved her time in the wilderness, but playing up this chapter in her life would later help her gain public sympathy and admiration as an artist.

This is an 1859 photo of Niagara Falls, as seen from Prospect Point in New York. Edmonia Lewis lived in the area with her brother and aunts after her parents died.

After her parents' deaths, Edmonia and her brother, Samuel, grew even closer. For approximately three years, the siblings lived an idyllic life among the Chippewa. She was known as "Wildfire" among them, and he was called "Sunrise." But one day, Samuel Lewis surprised his sister by telling her he planned to head to the West Coast. The California gold rush was under way, and he intended to seek his fortune in the faraway state.

Following his 1852 departure, Edmonia was reportedly left in the care of a Manhattan ship captain, leading to a period of intense loneliness over the next few years. She may have been a cheerful girl, but she was used to the slow pace of small towns, not of city life in Manhattan. When Edmonia became an artist, she did not provide many details about this lonely portion of her childhood.

Samuel Lewis

Samuel Lewis was born in 1835 in Haiti. He moved to the United States with his parents, but his father remarried after becoming a widower. Following the deaths of his father and stepmother, Samuel headed west in 1852 to strike it rich during the California gold rush. He opened up a barber shop in San Francisco and mined for gold.

He then traveled to Europe and, from there, headed back to the American West, living in Idaho and Montana. Lewis would lose $5,000 in gold after business failures and two of his buildings burned down.[5]

In 1868, he moved to Bozeman, Montana, and opened a barber shop. He was just one of ten blacks in the four-year-old city at that time. Fifteen years later, he built a home for himself on South Bozeman Avenue, now on the National Register of Historic Places. He also built four rental homes, two of which still exist.

In 1884, Lewis married Melissa Bruce and had a son with her.

After a brief illness, Samuel Lewis died on March 28, 1896.[6]

Samuel Lewis's home in Bozeman, Montana, is a historic landmark. He was one of the first African Americans in the state and grew to be a man of great influence and wealth.

College Life

Although Edmonia felt all alone when her brother left, his decision to head west paid off. Many gold seekers returned home empty-handed, but Samuel Lewis managed to find a fortune. He earned so much money from working as a barber and mining gold that he returned to Edmonia with enough cash to send his younger sister to school. According to some reports, she was educated by an order of black nuns.[7] Her brother then arranged for her to attend the New York Central College in McGrawville.

Edmonia Lewis had no idea that she'd entered one of the most forward-thinking colleges in the United States. Opened in 1849, McGrawville accepted male and female students of all racial backgrounds. In the nineteenth century, many academic institutions weren't this progressive. Most young women had to attend schools just for female students, and the options were even more limited for a woman of color like Edmonia Lewis, since colleges for whites typically barred nonwhites from entry. When Edmonia arrived at McGrawville in 1856, the college had roughly 120 students, including about 25 African Americans.

Little is known about Edmonia's studies at New York Central College. The institution folded not long after she left, and her academic records have not survived. But it's clear that she was exposed to both the fine arts and to the abolitionist community there.

The college was a stop on the Underground Railroad, the secret network of sites that helped enslaved blacks make their way to freedom. The "railroad" continued all the way to Canada, where slavery was illegal. Lewis had heard about the horrors of slavery, but her studies in college made

New York Central College, McGrawville

Edmonia Lewis was not the only student of color at New York Central College in McGrawville to become famous. Sisters Mary and Emily Edmondson attended the school after escaping slavery. The siblings became well-known abolitionists. Mahommah Baguagua also attended. Formerly enslaved by a ship captain, he ran away when the ship stopped in New York. His biography was published in 1854.[8]

New York Central College in McGrawville may have helped its students of color achieve prominence, but the school did not stay open. A smallpox outbreak, opposition to the school's mission, and financial difficulties led to the college closing in 1860. Afterward, it became a community school. Today, some of its buildings and a cemetery for African Americans remain there.[9]

her even more familiar with the practice that kept African Americans in bondage.

Although her time at New York Central College taught her much about the world, Lewis was not happy there. She may have been on the verge of dropping out when her brother persuaded her to transfer to Oberlin College in Ohio.

The Trials of Oberlin

When Edmonia Lewis arrived at Oberlin in fall 1859, the college (and the town it was named after) was one of the most liberal places in the United States. Oberlin admitted both men and women, blacks and whites, as students. And the city of Oberlin stood out for being racially integrated.

Studying at Oberlin

Established on September 2, 1833, Oberlin College decided to accept students of all racial backgrounds shortly after it

This is a 1905 image of Oberlin College, known for being one of the first US educational institutions to admit both whites and blacks.

opened. College trustee John Keep cast the final vote to institute a race-blind admissions policy at the school. He had a large home on the Oberlin campus, and Edmonia Lewis was one of the students who stayed there. But she had come to the right place at the wrong time.

Oberlin, Ohio, may have been more racially progressive than other towns, but it was also a community in crisis. It all stemmed from abolitionist John Brown's effort to take over the federal arsenal at Harpers Ferry, Virginia, in hopes of starting an armed slave revolt. Many Oberlin residents favored the raid, which ended in defeat and Brown's capture and trial. Others feared that the country's rising tensions concerning slavery would place Oberlin in danger since the town was part of the Underground Railroad and welcomed African Americans who'd escaped slavery.

John Brown, Radical Abolitionist

John Brown was born May 9, 1800, in Torrington, Connecticut. He grew up in a family that opposed slavery, but he didn't dedicate his life to fighting the institution until 1837.

In the 1850s, he and five of his sons moved to Kansas specifically to keep the territory slavery-free. On May 25, 1856, Brown and his sons killed five men after proslavery forces invaded Lawrence, Kansas, an abolitionist town. Brown lost a son in the fighting, which led to warfare throughout Kansas.

The next year, six abolitionists gave Brown money to carry out a slave revolt. On October 16, 1859, twenty-two men, including Brown, three of his sons, and five black men, raided the US military arsenal at Harpers Ferry, Virginia. They planned to use the weapons to start a rebellion.

But soldiers stopped Brown and his men from completing their plan. Ten men died during the conflict, including two of Brown's sons.

Brown survived but was found guilty of treason and murder on November 2, 1859, and sentenced to death. He was executed a month later.[1]

John Brown was a radical abolitionist who gave his life to stop the spread of slavery, but his actions divided the abolitionist community.

After John Brown was put to death in December 1859, Lewis was almost certainly present at the memorials held for him in Oberlin. These events celebrated Brown's life and activism, despite the abolitionist's execution and fears that Oberlin could come under attack due to the antislavery views of its residents.

During John Brown's raid on Harpers Ferry, Edmonia Lewis was simply a student trying to find her way at Oberlin College. Her skin color, however, made it impossible for her to escape the national debate over slavery. And two years later, as the nation became ensnared in the Civil War, she would find herself at the center of a conflict that heightened racial tensions.

A Terrible Accusation

In January 1862, Edmonia Lewis was accused of a terrible crime—poisoning two white classmates. It started on a cold January morning when Lewis invited the two students, who lived downstairs from her, to have a warm drink. Since the young women were about to go on a sleigh ride with two male friends, they welcomed the chance to have some spiced wine.

Lewis poured them a drink but did not have any herself, which would later seem suspicious. The students left her room without incident, but they became violently ill about an hour into their sleigh ride. They had to return to their parents' homes, where they remained sick for days. They accused Edmonia Lewis of poisoning them with cantharides, a toxic substance commonly called "Spanish fly."[2] The substance has a reputation for being an aphrodisiac, or sexual stimulant. In large doses, however, it can make people sick.

John Keep, who had years earlier cast the deciding vote to admit blacks and women to Oberlin, believed Edmonia Lewis was innocent. But community members remained unconvinced, and Lewis was viciously attacked when she briefly stepped outside the Keep house. According to Lewis, a mob blindfolded and badly beat her, leaving her in a cornfield nearly dead.[3]

When Lewis did not come to dinner or appear in time for bed, the bells of Oberlin rang. A search party was organized, and Lewis was found lying face down. Despite her condition, some of her critics accused her of exaggerating the seriousness of her injuries.

After her attack, Lewis was formally charged with poisoning her two classmates, but her friends found an attorney to help her. His name was John Mercer Langston and, like Lewis, he had both African American and Native American ancestry. He was also part white.

An 1849 Oberlin College graduate, Langston had become one of the community's most respected residents. But the charges against Edmonia Lewis had brought out the lingering racial tensions in the town. "No case ever tried in Oberlin or originating in that community, had ever produced such popular feeling as this,"[4] he later wrote.

Defending Lewis tested his skills as an attorney—and his dignity as a human being. When Langston went to examine one of the students allegedly sickened by Lewis's beverage, her father tried to shoot him. Fortunately, a fast-acting neighbor stopped the man and saved Langston's life.

John Mercer Langston

John Mercer Langston was born December 14, 1829, in Louisa County, Virginia, to a freedwoman of black and Native American ancestry and an English planter.

He earned a bachelor's degree from Oberlin College in 1849 and a master's degree in theology from the school three years later.

Shortly afterward, he began studying and practicing law. He and his two brothers were also active in the abolitionist movement and provided assistance to blacks fleeing slavery.

In 1868, he moved to Washington, DC, serving as dean of Howard University's law school, the first black law school in the country. He later served as US minister to Haiti and president of Virginia Normal and Collegiate Institute. In 1888, he ran for US Congress as a Republican. After contesting the election results due to voter fraud and intimidation, he won the race, becoming the first African American elected to Congress from Virginia.[5]

He died on November 15, 1897. Known for his political career, he was also the great-uncle of poet and writer Langston Hughes, born four years after his death.

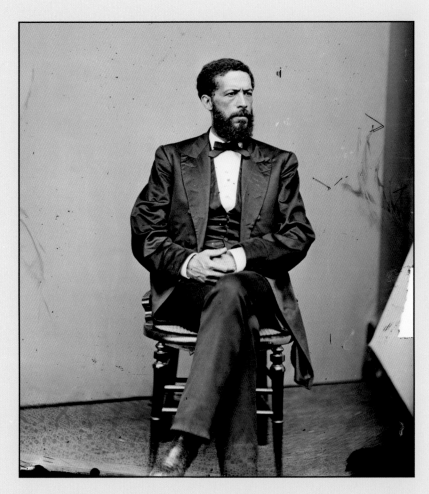

As a mixed-race African American, attorney John Mercer Langston could relate to Edmonia Lewis's struggles. He did his best to defend her, despite the risks doing so posed to him.

The Trial

When his client's trial began, Langston thought he was well-prepared to defend her, despite the fact that four attorneys came to work for the prosecution. The families of the sickened students were well-liked and respected, which many townspeople believed would lead to Lewis's conviction. Even the African American community was not in her corner because prior to the case she had interacted largely with the whites in town, Langston later recalled.

Although the attorneys for the prosecution presented a strong case, it was largely based on circumstantial evidence. To be sure, Lewis had given the students a warm drink, but the prosecution could not eliminate other possible reasons for their illness. After two days of testimony, the prosecution rested, and Langston presented his defense of Lewis.

He pointed out how poisoning by cantharides could only be proven with stool and urine samples, but none had been provided. He argued against the prosecutor's case on the basis of *corpus delecti*, a Latin term meaning that no hard evidence, such as a body or injuries, had been found.

It's unclear if Langston would have prevailed today, since forensic science is much more advanced. But for his time, the lawyer argued his case well enough for his client to be exonerated. The two-day hearing ended in dismissal of all charges. One account of the trial stated, "The orphan friendless young colored woman as many called her, who had been accused, perhaps without reason, and thus outraged without cause, was carried in the arms of her excited associates and fellow students from the courtroom…fully vindicated in her character and name."[6]

Legally, the trial was a success for Edmonia Lewis, but she had not been cleared in the court of public opinion. While she had many supporters, the situation had also given her enemies, some of whom had the power to alter her life at Oberlin.

Among the Abolitionists

Although Edmonia Lewis won a not-guilty verdict, she couldn't go back to her old life at Oberlin. Yes, she had her supporters, but a sizeable portion of the community continued to question her innocence. Those who didn't believe she intended to poison her classmates wondered if she wished to sexually excite them since Spanish fly was an aphrodisiac.[1] Even if that were the case, spiking people's drinks without their consent is still a crime.

Starting Over

Lewis's foes made life at Oberlin College miserable for her. She'd hear taunts of "poison" and "Spanish fly" when she passed by. And her reputation took another hit when she was accused of a different crime. Almost a year to the day after her beverage allegedly sickened her classmates, Lewis was accused of stealing art supplies.

Her accuser, a professor, had little evidence to support the claim and likely just wanted to see Lewis get what some community members thought she deserved. A hearing took place, however, and all charges against Lewis were dropped due to a lack of evidence. But this second incident truly ruined Oberlin for her.

The college registrar refused to enroll her for the fall semester of 1863. This was not the same as expulsion, but it had the same result since it prevented her from attending classes. Giving up on the idea of higher education, Lewis left town[2] and made her way to Boston. How she made it to the city remains unknown, but plenty of trains ran in that direction, and she probably boarded one with money from friends or from her brother.

Once she reached Boston, Lewis found it to be a friendly place for African Americans. Founded in 1630, the city was one of the oldest and most sophisticated in the United States. Manhattan had a bigger population, and Philadelphia had more wealth, but Boston was a cultural, intellectual, and artistic center. Lewis had chosen the right place.

Her brother had probably given her the money necessary to get settled in her new home. The invention of the transcontinental telegraph in 1861 allowed for fairly quick money transfers, so Samuel Lewis could have helped his sister financially without traveling to her in person. What's certain is that Edmonia Lewis soon had an art studio on Tremont Street, very close to where the Massachusetts State House stands today.

In addition to her brother, local abolitionists may have helped Lewis. She may have confided in them that she hoped to make fine art, but she kept the fact that she'd left Oberlin clouded by controversy a secret. She was still so

This early photo of Tremont Street shows what Boston looked like during the Victorian era. In this city, Edmonia Lewis launched her sculpting career.

hurt from her experiences at the college that she did not mention them to anyone during her two years in Boston.

Lewis may have been deprived of the chance to complete her studies at Oberlin, but in Boston, she willed herself to learn all she could about fine art. She started a short apprenticeship with Edward A. Brackett. Self-taught, he was not the best of Boston's sculptors, but he and Lewis worked fairly well together. At first, Brackett gave Lewis small tasks, but then he saw how well she'd modeled a foot in clay and knew she had real potential.

A photograph of Brackett from this time period reveals a rough-looking man who, perhaps, had seen many difficulties in life. But Brackett was also a socially conscious person who identified with the mission of abolitionist John Brown. Shortly before Brown's 1859 execution, Brackett traveled to the Virginia jail where the abolitionist was imprisoned. He made measurements of Brown's head and chest to create a sculpture of the activist. Brackett ended up making a fine bust of Brown in marble and later allowed Lewis to make Brown's bust in clay during her apprenticeship with him. Lewis did such a good job on her likeness of Brown that she made dozens of replicas, selling them at the Soldier's Relief Fair.

Capturing Colonel Shaw's Likeness

Lewis's busts of Brown launched her career as a sculptor. Afterward, she decided to sculpt the late colonel Robert Gould Shaw, who led black troops during the Civil War. But Lewis's acquaintances, including abolitionists Lydia Maria Child and William Lloyd Garrison as well as sculptors Ann Whitney and Harriet Hosmer, doubted she could pull

Lydia Maria Child

Lydia Maria Francis was born February 11, 1802, into a family of abolitionists in Medford, Massachusetts. In the 1820s, she taught and wrote fiction. She married editor David L. Child in 1828 and spent most of her married life fighting slavery.

In 1833, her most popular book, *An Appeal in Favor of That Class of Americans Called Africans*, was published. In it, she criticized how society had denied African Americans meaningful opportunities in life, especially related to schooling and work. Child faced a great deal of disapproval for the book, but her words influenced many readers to fight slavery.[3]

Child also edited the *National Anti-Slavery Standard*, a publication that ran from 1841 to 1843, and wrote down the accounts of freedmen and women about the horrors of human bondage. In addition to African Americans, she championed Native American causes.

She died October 20, 1880.

Lydia Maria Child used her writing and editing skills to spread the abolitionist cause. Her works swayed scores of white Americans to view slavery as wrong.

off the bust. Child, in particular, had never encountered someone like Edmonia Lewis before and didn't know what to make of her.

"To my mind there is something peculiarly interesting in the fact that this little Edmonia comes from basket-weaving and moccasin-embroidery in lonely forests among the Chippewas, to live shut up in a little studio [in Boston],"[4] Lydia Maria Child wrote.

Child's description of Lewis as "little" seems somewhat patronizing, but the budding sculptor was both physically small and a young woman. Since Child was forty-two years older than the artist, she may not have used the adjective as an insult of Lewis, who had also spoken openly about her childhood in the wilderness with her mother's people. Growing up in nature had influenced Lewis to become an artist, and Child believed in her abilities. She wrote that Lewis was special and blessed with a clear desire to work toward her goals. Still, sculpting was one of the most difficult and demanding of the fine arts, so Child wondered if Lewis could make it in the field, especially without formal training.

"I, with my sixty years of observation, knew better than she could what a long and difficult hill she had to climb before she could reach the summit of her Art,"[5] Child later recalled.

By choosing to sculpt Colonel Shaw, a man she'd never met, Lewis may have made her work all the more challenging, Child feared.[6] Only a gifted artist could sculpt Shaw realistically without having met him, but Lewis had a gift. When Child first set eyes on Lewis's bust of him,

Edmonia Lewis launched her career with the support of abolitionists. In response, she sculpted subjects such as the war hero Robert Gould Shaw, a hero to that community.

Robert Gould Shaw

Robert Gould Shaw was born October 10, 1837, in Boston. He came from a wealthy family of abolitionists, widely respected in society. He attended European boarding schools but expressed a desire to return to the United States to fight in the military.

In 1861, he joined the New York militia. Two years later, he accepted the challenge of leading the Civil War's first regiment of African American soldiers, the Fifty-Fourth Massachusetts Regiment, which included Frederick Douglass's sons Charles and Lewis Douglass. Shaw had hesitated to take the job but was soon impressed by the black soldiers in his command. When they boycotted their pay after learning they received less for their service than white soldiers, Shaw joined them in the boycott until the policy was changed.[9]

Tragically, Shaw died on July 18, 1863, while leading his men in an attack on Confederate Fort Wagner, just outside Charleston, South Carolina. He was twenty-five.

she was pleasantly surprised. The abolitionist observed that Lewis had "wrought well with her unpracticed hand."[7]

As Child stood in Lewis's studio, she examined the work in clay. She found the features truly resembled the fallen hero, and she was touched by one move Lewis made in particular. Noticing that the clay was drying out, Lewis took water from a vase and lovingly sprinkled the head with care.[8] This act convinced Child that she stood in the presence of a true artist.

Edmonia Lewis happened to take off as an artist in Boston during a time when the city developed a great interest in Africa. Artists were creating works about the continent, and writers were composing speeches about it. Boston's William Wetmore Story sculpted *The African Sybill*, and New Englander Anne Whitney sculpted *Africa Waking from Sleep*. But both of these artists were white. Lewis stood out because she was black and Native American and had the talent necessary to compose compelling pieces of art.

She made a large enough profit from sculpting that she began to consider a move overseas. Relocating to Europe would give her a chance to educate herself about art in a way that she could not in the United States. In Italy, particularly, she could learn how the classical artists had traditionally approached sculpture. With a brother on the West Coast and her parents long gone, Lewis had little reason to remain in her native country.

5

To the Eternal City

Edmonia Lewis kept her plans to leave Boston private at first. Although she felt she could do better in another city, she did not wish to lose the friendship of her patrons. While Boston offered American artists many opportunities, European cities such as London, Paris, and Rome offered even more. An American artist could really thrive abroad, and Rome was already home to a community of US expatriates, including sculptors. So, Lewis decided that Italy was the country for her.

She may have raised the money for the trip from her earnings selling busts, but her brother may have helped her make the move, just as he'd supported her previously. Lewis did not have a tendency to splurge, so she may very well have saved the funds necessary to travel abroad.

Life in Italy

In August 1865, Lewis left Boston for Europe. She first arrived in England, spending time in London. Then, she traveled to Paris. From there, she headed to Florence, Italy. The abolitionist newspaper *The Liberator* alerted its readers to the progress of Lewis's journey by publishing an account that it picked up from the *Boston Commonwealth*. *The Liberator* quoted:

> MISS EDMONIA LEWIS AT FLORENCE. Our readers will be pleased to learn that, through the kind offices of Mr. M. Perry Kennard, of this city, (who attended to her finances, secured her a stateroom, gave her written directions for travelling on the Continent,(&c.,) this young lady reached Florence after a very agreeable passage across the Atlantic and through Paris. At Florence, Mr. Marsh, our minister, and his lady, showed her many attentions; our townsman, Mr. Thomas Ball, the sculptor, furnished her with several tools; Mr. Powers a moulding-block; and other friends were equally kind. In contrast with this generosity should be mentioned the conduct of a Boston lady there residing, who, when Edmonia sent in a letter of introduction given by her own sister in this city, returned it to her, and declined to receive her. – because she was "colored".! – *Boston Commonwealth*.[1]

Lewis was welcomed in Florence. The US minister to Italy, George Perkins Marsh, was friendly to the young artist, as was Vermont-born sculptor Hiram S. Powers. His *The Greek Slave* was considered the finest piece of sculpture made by an American at the time. Powers had finished the first version of his masterpiece in 1844 and then preceded to make five not-quite-identical copies. Between 1847 and

In 1846, Hiram Powers completed this version of *The Greek Slave*, displayed here at the Corcoran Gallery of Art in Washington, DC.

1851, two versions of the statue were exhibited as part of a tour across the eastern United States.[2]

Lewis also had the support of Thomas Ball, one of the best sculptors of the period. His statue of George Washington had recently been placed on Boston Common. But Lewis's stay in Florence was just a temporary stop on her way to Rome, where she moved by the end of the year.

As a newcomer to Rome, Lewis didn't know what the city once looked like, but it had fallen on hard times by the 1860s. Two generations earlier, Rome had been prosperous and clean, but Lewis saw a city that looked rundown following a series of conflicts and wars. Only when examining the ancient statues and architecture there did one detect the city's former greatness.

Rome's history was enough to attract prominent Americans to relocate there, however. One such American, Bostonian William Wetmore Story, was a leader of the city's expatriate community. His father, Joseph Story, became a US Supreme Court justice, but William Story preferred art to law. Talkative and sociable, he connected with the group of Americans who'd moved to Rome after relocating to the city himself in 1850. When Edmonia Lewis arrived, Story had been widely praised for his sculpture *Cleopatra*, a new take on the Egyptian queen.

Along with Story, actress Charlotte Cushman became a leader of the American expatriates in Rome. She was born and raised in Boston, like Story, and yearned to live in a city where her artistic qualities would be more appreciated. After leaving home at an early age, Cushman moved to New York City and then to London. In both cities, she was hailed as one of the finest actresses of her

Story's Cleopatra

William Wetmore Story used white Italian marble for his 1858 sculpture *Cleopatra*. The work approaches Cleopatra as a complex ruler rather than just a beautiful queen.[3]

In the piece, Cleopatra ponders her death, which she will experience when she allows the asp, a poisonous snake, to bite her. To suggest this, Story included a snake charm wrapped around the queen's wrist, along with other jewelry, such as a pearl necklace and a bangle.

The scholars who've examined the sculpture have marveled at its symmetry and how well it was made overall. Story's *Cleopatra* marked a new chapter for American sculptors. It showed that they could be just as skillful as the Europeans.

Born in 1819, William Wetmore Story was a sculptor, art critic, poet, and editor from Massachusetts. He is most famous for his sculpture *Cleopatra*, which also inspired Edmonia Lewis.

Charlotte Saunders Cushman was a stage actress and a leader of the group of American expatriate artists in Rome. Edmonia Lewis was part of this circle but never quite fit in as the sole woman of color.

time. In the nineteenth century, male actors dominated the stage, but Cushman was such a good actress that she could play both male and female roles. Her deep voice certainly helped in this regard.

In Rome, Cushman was the center of a group of about twelve American female expatriates. The group included the New Yorker Emma Stebbins and the Bostonian Harriet Goodhue Hosmer, a celebrated sculptor. All of these women had been involved in same-sex relationships. While Cushman and Stebbins had been romantically involved, Hosmer was Cushman's romantic rival. Edmonia Lewis is believed to have had same-sex relationships as well, but with whom remains a mystery.

In Hosmer, Lewis found a female role model. Hosmer enjoyed the hard work of molding clay and marble, and her piece *Zenobia in Chains* showed that women could excel as sculptors. Now in the Wadsworth Atheneum Museum of Art in Hartford, Connecticut, the sculpture depicts Queen Zenobia of the Palmyrene Empire as a proud leader, even as she's placed in chains by her Roman captors. The sculpture was a breakthrough for American conceptual sculpture, but the finished work is also a masterpiece.

Hosmer relied on a team of Italians to help her with her sculptures, and in one photo, she poses with these men

Harriet Hosmer

Harriet Hosmer was born October 9, 1830, in Watertown, Massachusetts. Her physician father, Hiram Hosmer, encouraged her to study anatomy and art. She arrived in Rome in 1853 and became involved with a colony of artists and writers that included Nathaniel Hawthorne and Elizabeth Barrett Browning. There, Hosmer seriously began to study sculpture.[4]

Her interest in mythology influenced her work, the bulk of which was large-scale sculpture in the neoclassical tradition. Working on big sculptures countered ideas of what women artists could accomplish. And Hosmer's romantic relationships with women challenged societal norms as well.

Hosmer died in 1908 at the age of seventy-seven.

Sculptor Harriet Goodhue Hosmer completed the marble sculpture *Zenobia in Chains* in 1859.

to honor them. She clearly had the strength to do much of the work, but it helped to have these assistants.

Inspired by women such as Hosmer and her new surroundings, Edmonia Lewis quickly set up an art studio. After sculpting busts of an abolitionist and a Civil War hero in Boston, she was ready to give high art a try. This ambition would lead her to become the first African American and Native American woman to succeed internationally as a neoclassical sculptor.

6

A Shift in Focus

"**O**f the lady artists in Rome, less is known than should be."[1]

These are the opening words to an 1866 essay in the prestigious London-based *Art Journal*. The author, Henry Wreford, listed the artistic achievements of several women in the piece and was struck by the number of American artists among them. While he commented on the technical skill of various US expatriates, he took a special interest in Edmonia Lewis, who had arrived in Rome a few months earlier.

An Artist of Interest

Wreford found Lewis fascinating, describing her as a child of the forest who preferred the wilderness to city life. He said that her "sex, extreme youth, and color, enlist our warmest sympathies."[2] His interest in Lewis had partly been inspired by the artist herself. She had publicly discussed her longing for a life in the woods but said that her love of sculpture prevented her from living as she had years ago.[3] Lewis recognized that art reviewers enjoyed hearing about her childhood years among the Chippewa, and she used sculpture to discuss both her indigenous and African American heritage.

Wreford, for example, wrote about an antislavery sculpture Lewis made that has since been lost. "The first ideal of our young artist is a freed woman falling on her knees, and with clasped hands and uplifted eyes thanking God for the blessings of liberty," he commented. "She had not forgotten her people, and this early delineation of her genius to their cause is honorable to their feelings."[4]

Using Sculpture to Discuss Ideas

Since sculpting requires a great deal of physical strength, it is one of the most difficult of the fine arts. For sculptors, tasks such as cutting marble posed challenges, but assistants could offset some of these issues.

Sculpture is not only difficult because of the strength it requires but also because it's not easy to correct mistakes. When errors are made, the sculptor simply has to keep going. But the artform also has its advantages. Artists can use it to express concepts, or ideas. In *Forever Free*, for instance, Edmonia Lewis used sculpture to show the deep feelings of appreciation African Americans had after getting their freedom. While a painting can certainly capture emotion as well, the flatness of canvas prevents it from expressing feeling in the three-dimensional way that sculpture can.

At this point, Lewis had already sculpted John Brown and Robert Gould Shaw, both white men. Newly in Rome, she was interested in using art to portray African Americans and Native Americans. The young and untrained artist had managed to create sculpture after sculpture. But how did she get so much done? Lewis generally didn't answer this question, but working in silence certainly helped her create a large body of work in a short amount of time. Her new sculptures included her most ambitious project yet, *Forever Free*, unveiled in 1867.

Now part of the Smithsonian American Art Museum's permanent collection, *Forever Free* shows a woman on her knees with her hands clasped and her head tilted up, as if thanking God. The work also includes a black man standing with one hand lifted in victory. Because President Abraham Lincoln's Emancipation Proclamation includes the phrase "forever free," it's clear the figures in the sculpture are grateful to be free from slavery, but the fact that a woman of color created the sculpture adds more emotion to the work.

As remarkable a work as *Forever Free* is, it caused controversy for Lewis. While most artists didn't make marble sculptures unless hired to first, she carved her piece without a commission, or contract. To make matters worse, Lewis sent the sculpture to a wealthy Boston abolitionist named Samuel E. Sewell, who had no idea the shipment was coming. Once it arrived, he had to pay a thousand dollars in shipping and other fees, an enormous amount of money in the nineteenth century.[5] Although he managed to raise the money, he resented Lewis for sending him the sculpture without okaying it with him beforehand.

An 1880 photograph features sculptor Anne Whitney. She made busts of historical and political figures. She knew Edmonia Lewis but found her to be unusual.

Word about this spread throughout Boston, leading some community members there to rethink their support of her.

Redeeming Herself

Edmonia Lewis had unknowingly created tension between herself and her Boston supporters, and she did not quite fit in with the community of women artists in Rome. Her skin color set her apart from the rest of them, and some of the women, such as artist Anne Whitney, found Lewis to be strange. She wrote to a friend: "Edmonia is a queer little creature, but [also] very kind and obliging. She saw the [French soldiers] making their entrance [to Rome] and felt a good deal excited about it. A lady standing next to her asked, 'Where are they going?' 'To the devil,' answered Edmonia with a great swing of her arm which caused her to lose her balance and tumble into a hole as deep as herself."[6]

Perhaps Lewis was clumsy and unsure of herself, but that Whitney described the incident at all and referred to her as "queer" likely meant that the young black woman hadn't been fully embraced by the circle of American women artists in Rome.

Forming friendships in a place where few people looked like her may have been difficult, but Lewis always had her work. The subject of slavery was still on her mind, but for her next piece, Lewis turned to the Old Testament for inspiration rather than the United States. In 1868, she began sculpting a work called *Hagar in the Wilderness*, named after the handmaid of Sarah, wife of Jewish patriarch Abraham.

Abraham and Sarah desperately wanted to have a child, but Sarah feared the opportunity had passed them by because they were already very old. So, Sarah arranged for Hagar to be a surrogate mother of sorts for her. Abraham would get Hagar pregnant, but Sarah would be considered the child's mother. Once the baby was born, however, Sarah and Hagar began to fight, and Sarah had her and the child thrown out of their home and into the wilderness.

A Bust of Edmonia Lewis

Edmonia Lewis didn't just create busts, she sat for an artist to have her own bust made. In 1870, the *Art Journal* described how British artist Isabel Curtis-Cholmeley, an expatriate in Rome, had made a sculpture of Lewis.[7] This work indicates that at least one fellow artist saw the importance of capturing Lewis in clay.

Cholmeley and Lewis were reportedly best friends, but Cholmeley would move from Rome to Venice and sculpt as Contessa Isabel Curtis-Cholmeley after marrying an Italian government official. Unfortunately, the bust has since been lost, but a select group of photos reveal what Lewis looked like. While seven of these pictures, taken by Chicago photographer Henry Roche, had already been identified as Lewis, an eighth photo of her turned up in 2011.[8] That year, Jacqueline Copeland of the Walters Art Museum found the undiscovered picture of the artist in a Baltimore antique shop.

"Oh my God, this is Edmonia Lewis!" she shouted. The photo was traced back to a studio in Rome. It gives art lovers another view of Lewis, who appears in the image wearing a ruffled Victorian gown.

Edmonia Lewis's 1868 sculpture *Hagar* was a tribute to the enslaved woman in the Bible who fled into the wilderness with her child.

Orphaned as a small child with no real place to call home afterward, Lewis related to the biblical story. Many African American women saw themselves in Hagar, as they, too, had been enslaved and exploited.

Lewis cast *Hagar* in clay, but a marble version, cut years later, is now part of the Smithsonian American Art Museum's permanent collection. *Hagar* is not a masterpiece but stands out as a work of an artist on her way to mastery. The fine lines and emotion in the sculpture all point to Lewis's talent, which had improved greatly since she first started out in Boston. But Lewis still had a long way to go before she would achieve true greatness.

After using sculpture to highlight the lives of abolitionists and the enslaved in her work, Lewis would next use her art to highlight her Native American ancestry. This shift would draw even more attention to Lewis.

Chapter 7

Longfellow and Hiawatha

Edmonia Lewis had a deep appreciation for Henry Wadsworth Longfellow, one of the most admired poets of her time. Born and raised in Maine, Longfellow had written about the New England Puritans of two centuries earlier. Today, his poem "The Midnight Ride of Paul Revere" remains popular, but the epic poem "The Song of Hiawatha" was the most famous Longfellow work during his lifetime. The poem chronicles the indigenous peoples of the Great Lakes region.

Reading Longfellow

First published in 1855, "Hiawatha" helped white Americans better understand the Native American population. The work offers an emotional take on the thousands of American Indians who lost their lives after Europeans colonized the Americas. It predicts that the indigenous peoples of the United States will one day be

The work of Henry Wadsworth Longfellow inspired Edmonia Lewis's sculpture *The Marriage of Hiawatha*. This is a photo of the poet and novelist taken circa 1870.

wiped out. While wars with Europeans and the diseases they brought to the Americas resulted in the deaths of thousands of native people, the indigenous population is very much present in the twenty-first century. But no one knew what would become of Native Americans in the 1800s, and Lewis admired Longfellow's work.

In 1867's *Book of the Artists*, which chronicled fine artists, including the American expatriates in Rome, a reporter discussed Lewis's reading habits.

"She has read 'Evangeline,' and some others of Longfellow's poems, and has caught from them a girlish sentimentality,"[1] the reporter wrote. "By and by, when her horizon of knowledge becomes more expanded, and her grasp on it firmer, she will leave the prettiness of poems,

Native Americans in Art

In 1855, the year Longfellow's "Hiawatha" was published, images of Native Americans were few and far between. George Catlin's paintings stood out as a major exception.

Born in Pennsylvania in 1796, Catlin took his first trip to the West in 1830. He then made Native Americans the focus of much of his artwork. Catlin mostly painted the indigenous peoples of the western United States, so his viewers came to know the Great Plains Indians while remaining ignorant of the Native Americans who lived in the Eastern Woodlands. Edmonia Lewis belonged to this group.

and give us Pocahontas, Logan, Pontiac, Tecumseh, Red Jacket, and, it may be, Black Hawk and Osceola."[2]

The writer also characterized Lewis as a "little American girl,"[3] but he believed she had the potential to sculpt great works of art, using famous indigenous people such as Montezuma, Atahualpa, and La Malinche as subjects. These historical figures all played roles in the Spanish conquest of Mexico.

A Chance Encounter

In 1868, Longfellow and his family traveled to Rome. This offered Lewis the chance to meet her idol in person, but meeting him seemed impossible because the author was so famous that his time in Rome had been tightly scheduled. Eager to make a bust of his face, Lewis secretly followed him around town so she could get a better idea of what he looked like. Before long, the artist was working on her bust of her favorite poet.

One day, Samuel Longfellow, the poet's brother, happened to stop by Lewis's studio. Noticing a fresh bust of his brother, Samuel was so delighted that he ran out to get the rest of his family, including Longfellow himself. The poet finally ended up sitting for Lewis, and she completed a fine bust of him in clay. Once funds were raised in Boston, she finished another Longfellow bust in marble.

Even before she met and sculpted Longfellow, Lewis had been fascinated by his poetic references to Native Americans. In 1867, she had sculpted *The Old Arrow Maker and His Daughter*, now in the permanent collection of the Smithsonian American Art Museum. In this sculpture, the father crouches to the viewer's right, and his daughter

Transatlantic Communication

The debut of the transatlantic telegraph cable in 1858 made it possible for people on opposite sides of the Atlantic Ocean to contact each other more quickly than ever before. The undersea cable allowed for text or symbols to be transmitted without exchanging a piece of paper or another item featuring the message. Rather than delivering a message by ship, which could take ten days, these cables allowed information to be shared in minutes.

The efficiency of the transatlantic telegraph cable allowed Edmonia Lewis to quickly raise the funds needed for a huge Longfellow bust in marble.[4] This effort took only a matter of months. Today, Lewis's marble bust of Longfellow is at Harvard University.

to the viewer's left. Both wear necklaces, and the lace or trim of their garments suggest they are wealthy. The father holds a chisel in his right hand as he gestures to his left to guide his daughter. She, however, gazes straight ahead at the viewer. In this piece, Lewis engages viewers by bringing them into the world of a Native American family.

Lewis followed up that sculpture with *The Marriage of Hiawatha*. Also cast in white marble, *The Marriage* is not as visually compelling, but it tells an important story about the love between Hiawatha and Minnehaha. Hands locked, Hiawatha and Minnehaha stare at each other.

Proud of her Native American heritage, Edmonia Lewis used the sculpture *The Old Arrow Maker* to defy stereotypes of Native Americans. It portrayed them as a dignified people.

The stonework is not as well done as *The Old Arrow Maker*, but the work, like many of Lewis's, tapped into the emotions of viewers.

Today, Lewis's works *Hagar* and *Forever Free* are much better known than *The Marriage of Hiawatha* and *The Old Arrow Maker*. More than a century and a half later, though, her Native American sculptures still deserve attention.

Trips Back Home

After a few years in Rome, Edmonia Lewis considered the city her home. The Eternal City was the source of much of her artistic inspiration, and her fellow American expatriates sometimes made Lewis feel as if she was part of something larger than herself. But she had also turned to religion during her time in the Roman Catholic city.

Embracing Catholicism

The United States was by and large a Protestant country, but Lewis had been exposed to Catholicism likely when an order of black nuns had educated her during her childhood. Scholars believe the Chippewa side of her family may have also been Catholic. Exposure to the religion during her youth likely led to her later embracing the faith, which she publicly committed to at some point in the late 1860s.

Some of the artists in her circle questioned Lewis's involvement in the religion. Sculptor Anne Whitney wondered if Lewis turned to Catholicism in hopes of landing more work in a country where the religion was widely practiced.

"Edmonia Lewis has turned Catholic and her reasons for it are better than her Catholicism," Whitney wrote a friend. "The American clergyman took no notice of her and her Catholic acquaintances were very friendly."[1]

This criticism seems unfair, given that Lewis's connection to the religion dated back to her childhood. It also shows that the women artists in Rome weren't very supportive of the sole woman of color among them. That said, Lewis's Catholicism did bring her new business. In 1868, she met John Patrick Crichton Stuart, the third Marquess of Bute. He was in Rome after his recent conversion to Catholicism. Stuart was very wealthy and bought an altarpiece of the *Madonna and Child* from Lewis for three thousand pounds, which would be roughly $440,930 today.

The large commission and the patronage of such an important man marked a turning point for Lewis. The money she made from *Madonna and Child*, now lost, allowed her to pay off her debts. The interest noblemen like Stuart took in her work also caused people to treat Lewis with more respect.

"Why, I am invited everywhere, and am treated just as nicely as if the bluest of blue blood flowed through my veins," she said. "I number among my patrons the Marquis [sic] of Bute, Lady Ashburton and other members of the nobility."[2]

Madonna and Child has since been lost, as have many of Lewis's religious sculptures.

Lost and Found

Although a number of Lewis's religious works have been lost or destroyed, a bust of Jesus Christ she made for Stuart was found in the Bute family collection in 2015, roughly 140 years after its completion. Historians and biographers had mostly given up any hope of recovering the work, which is not that striking, as Lewis sculpted Christ very much as he's described in the Bible. Perhaps that's what Stuart wanted, however. A new take on Christ might not have gone over well.

While Lewis's bust of Jesus Christ has been found, others she made for Stuart were lost in an 1877 fire on the grounds of Mount Stuart, home of the marquesses of Bute.[3]

This image depicts the 1872 marriage of the Marquess of Bute in London, England. Edmonia Lewis's bust of Jesus Christ was in the Bute family collection.

Return to the United States

Having made a name for herself in Europe, Lewis returned to the United States in 1870 and brought several pieces of art with her. She intended to pay for her travels by selling her works and had reportedly told a government worker that she had brought twenty thousand dollars of art across the ocean. But Lewis didn't sell as much as she'd hoped.

That wasn't the only disappointment of the artist's American trip. Her brother, Samuel, was living in Montana, so she did not reunite with him. A few years later, however, Lewis returned to the United States with plans to travel to the American West.

In fall 1872, Lewis visited New York City and headed to the West Coast the following spring. The transcontinental railroad had only been completed four years earlier, and few women traveled cross-country alone. Lewis was not intimidated, however, and took a handful of sculptures with her to San Francisco, where she held a major art show.

When reporters asked why she had traveled so far, Lewis replied that the East Coast artists were not very friendly. They seemed to think embracing her would cause their own sales to drop. The West Coast, on the other hand, needed new artists and works of art.

Lewis didn't unload as many sculptures as she thought she would. She sold just three pieces of art—at lower prices than she'd hoped. And once again, she left without seeing her brother. He remained in Montana, unable to travel because he was recovering from a gunshot wound to his hand.

Edmonia completed her marble sculpture *Asleep* in 1871. It is now in the San Jose Public Library's collection.

The Transcontinental Railroad

The Pacific Railway Act of 1862 made it possible for the Central Pacific and Union Pacific railroads to get the resources needed to build a railroad across the country. The Central Pacific began the project by laying track in Sacramento, California, and continuing eastward. The Union Pacific began by laying track in Omaha, Nebraska, and continuing westward.

Central Pacific hired thousands of Chinese workers to build the railroad, a dangerous task in areas such as the Sierra Nevada mountains. Union Pacific turned largely to Irish immigrants to lay track, who did so in dangerous areas like the Rocky Mountains.

The rail lines met in Promontory, Utah, on May 10, 1869, after 1,800 miles (2,897 kilometers) of new track had been put down. From then on, Americans could travel cross-country by train in two weeks, a trip that had once taken six months.[4]

In the twenty-first century, Edmonia Lewis's presence can still be felt on the West Coast. Her sculptures *Awake* and *Asleep* were sold to a private collector who later donated them to the San Jose Public Library, where they remain today.

Edmonia Lewis never saw her brother again, but just as he did, she left her mark on the West. He left historic homes in the region, and she left her artwork there.

Cleopatra

After returning to Rome in 1873, Edmonia Lewis found that the American expatriate community was deeply interested in the Centennial International Exposition taking place in the summer of 1876. America's one-hundredth birthday party wasn't just a great opportunity for inventors to show off their wares but for artists, too. The event was their chance to shine.

Sculpting the African Queen

As the sole woman of color among Rome's community of American artists, Edmonia Lewis had never really belonged. Over time, she interacted with these expatriates less and less. The 1876 death of actress Charlotte Cushman marked the group's decline, as she had been one of its leaders. Lewis felt very much alone after the actress, who'd been friendly to her, died.

Still driven to create great art, however, Lewis hoped to make the best sculpture of her career. Sculptor William Wetmore Story had received a great deal of attention for his work *Cleopatra*, which showed the Egyptian queen

Sculptor William Wetmore Story's 1858 piece *Cleopatra* showed the Egyptian queen contemplating her death.

pondering her death. But Lewis believed she could offer a different perspective of the legendary ruler. She would present Cleopatra actually dying.

The Centennial Exposition opened in Philadelphia in May 1876 and included lions, elephants, and other exotic animals as well as machines such as Alexander Graham Bell's crude telephone. Paintings and sculpture were also displayed, and Edmonia Lewis couldn't wait to find out

Finding Cleopatra

After the Centennial Exposition in Philadelphia, Lewis exhibited *Death of Cleopatra* at the 1878 Interstate Industrial Exposition in Chicago, where she left it in storage.

At some point, gambler "Blind John" Condon bought the statue from a saloon and used it as a grave marker for a racehorse called Cleopatra. The sculpture remained at the site, in Chicago suburb Forest Park, for almost a century. But when the US Postal Service bought the racetrack land, the statue ended up in a storage yard, where it was damaged. The Forest Park Historical Society moved the sculpture into private storage and later donated it to the Smithsonian American Art Museum in 1994.[1]

The Smithsonian made roughly $30,000 of repairs to the statue, restoring *Cleopatra* to almost mint condition.

how the crowd would respond to her *Death of Cleopatra* piece. Had her sculpture outdone Story's version?

Her *Cleopatra* offered a, then, shocking version of the queen—head back in anguish as a snake's venom enters her bloodstream. The dying Cleopatra's breast is exposed, and her hand droops to her side. This version of the queen had never been presented to the public, and reactions to the work were mixed. Most critics acknowledged that Lewis had outdone herself with the sculpture, but some disliked seeing a dying, partly undressed Cleopatra.

Lewis's controversial take on Cleopatra did not just draw attention to the sculpture but to the artist herself. One reviewer described Lewis as a "bright and busy little creature"[2] who had arrived early in the morning to dust off her sculpture and prepare for the day. The critic went on to say that when Lewis was shown a letter written by George Washington, she asked for it to be pressed against her forehead,[3] as if she believed the note would cause some of the first president's greatness to rub off on her. And the *Daily Graphic*, a Philadelphia newspaper, quoted Lewis's interaction with a wealthy woman who objected to her *Cleopatra* sculpture.

The woman told her, "Miss Lewis, that is a very beautiful statue, but don't you think it would have been more proper to drape it." She went on to suggest that Cleopatra needed to be clothed for Christianity's sake. But Lewis responded, "Madame, that is not modesty in you. That is worse than mock modesty. You see and think of evil not intended. Your mind, Madame, is not as pure, I fear, as my statue."[4]

Edmonia Lewis's *Death of Cleopatra* sculpture was considered somewhat controversial. It showed the queen dying rather than just thinking about her death, as William Wetmore Story's sculpture had.

This quote was printed in nearly a dozen newspapers in the summer of 1876, making it the best-known story about Edmonia Lewis. Although her sculpture sparked lots of talk at the exposition, Lewis did not sell *Cleopatra*. Unable to send the sculpture back to Rome, she left it in the United States as she left for Italy once more.

Grant's World Tour

Ulysses S. Grant served as president from 1869 to 1877, but corruption scandals had shadowed his time in the White House. He'd also found it difficult to bring the North and South together after the Civil War. As his presidency ended, Grant badly needed a vacation and embarked on a world tour on May 17, 1877.

The highest British leaders, including Queen Victoria, welcomed him. From England, the Grants traveled to countries such as Belgium, Switzerland, Germany, and Denmark, consistently getting an enthusiastic welcome. The Europeans didn't view him as a corrupt president but as the military general who'd helped unite the United States following the Civil War.

The Grants also traveled to Egypt and the Middle East and returned to Europe to tour Greece and Italy, where the president met Edmonia Lewis. Afterward, the family headed to Asia, where Grant reportedly became the first person to shake Japanese emperor Mutsuhito's hand.

On December 16, 1879, President Grant and his family returned to the United States.[5]

New Opportunities Arise

The following year, Lewis experienced some career highlights. Former US president Ulysses S. Grant visited Italy as part of a world tour, and he commissioned Lewis to make a bust of his head. The president was pleased with her work, which she finished in 1878. That year, she also sculpted a bust of another high-profile client, John Cardinal McCloskey, the Roman Catholic Church's first American cardinal. Before his death in 1878, Pope Pius IX is said to have visited Lewis as well. The visit must have been a source of pride for a Catholic such as Lewis.

In 1879, Lewis returned to the United States, visiting both the East Coast and the Midwest. She hoped to sell her statue *The Veiled Bride of Spring*, based on the Roman goddess Flora.

Newspaper reports indicate that Lewis first visited Syracuse, New York, and then traveled to Cincinnati, Ohio. She sold *The Veiled Bride* at the Grand Bazaar, a Roman Catholic venue, in that city.

Lewis probably hoped that she'd be able to sell much more of her work in the United States, but that didn't turn out to be the case. There was no longer much of a demand for neoclassical sculptures in the States. By the 1880s, that style of art fell out of style, and Edmonia Lewis faded from the public eye, though she continued to sculpt.

Lewis's Legacy

Edmonia Lewis rarely appeared in the press after 1880. Because her brother continued to support her work, her name sometimes appeared in Montana newspapers, but she no longer garnered the media attention she once did from the nation's top publications, such as the *New York Times*. Not yet forty, Lewis's most successful years as an artist were behind her.

Fading from the Spotlight

But as her name slipped from the headlines, Lewis continued to have patrons. Her experience sculpting altarpieces gave her a following among Roman Catholics. During this time, however, she stopped writing to her friends in the United States and remained on the fringes of the group of women expatriates in Rome. In the 1890s, Lewis left Rome for Paris, continuing to sculpt in the French city. She created a bronze bust of the enslaved poet Phillis Wheatley that was displayed at the World's Columbian Exposition in Chicago. Her bust *Hiawatha* was also exhibited there. And in 1895,

Phillis Wheatley

Phillis Wheatley was born circa 1754. She is known for being the first African American and the first enslaved person to write a book of poetry. She was just the third American woman to achieve this.[1]

Born in West Africa, she was kidnapped, enslaved, and shipped to Boston, Massachusetts, in 1761. There, a man named John Wheatley purchased her to be a servant for his wife, Susannah. Phillis was very intelligent, quickly learning and reading English. Enslaved blacks were typically forbidden to read, but the Wheatleys encouraged Phillis to study, especially religion and English, Latin, and Greek literature.

Phillis published her first poem in 1767 and the book *Poems on Various Subjects* six years later. At that time, 1773, John Wheatley freed her from slavery.

She became world famous, counting President George Washington and French philosopher Voltaire among her fans.

But Phillis Wheatley struggled after her marriage to John Peters, a free man of color, in 1778. She could not find a publisher for her second poetry book. Sickly throughout her life, she died in 1784.[2]

a Lewis fan exhibited her sculpture of abolitionist senator Charles Sumner at the Atlanta World's Fair.[3]

The next year, Samuel Lewis died in Bozeman, Montana, after a brief illness. Though she had not seen her brother in decades, his passing meant that Lewis was truly all alone in the world. A successful businessman, Lewis left his sister some money, which probably proved helpful as her sculpting career slowed down.

For the final time, Lewis traveled to the United States, visiting New York and Chicago as the 1890s drew to a close. Back in Europe, the artist moved from Paris to London in 1901, but her health began to suffer and she wrote a will in 1905. Two years later, she was hospitalized in the Hammersmith neighborhood of London and died on September 19, 1907, at the age of sixty-three. She'd been suffering from a condition called Bright's disease, which causes the kidneys to swell. Lewis described herself as a "spinster and sculptor" in her will.[4]

Remembering Edmonia Lewis

Edmonia Lewis had lived a remarkable life, one without a single peer. As the first sculptor of African American and Native American ancestry to rise to international fame, Lewis was a trailblazer. She had no sculptors of color to confide in as she lived in Rome, an isolating experience. The women expatriates didn't fully accept her, and her brother lived in the American West, but Lewis could always turn to her art for companionship.

For decades after her death, both Lewis and her sculptures were forgotten. It wasn't until the 1960s, when there was a push to rediscover the works of artists of color,

More than a century after her death, interest in the sculptures of Edmonia Lewis has picked up again. She is no longer a forgotten artist.

that interest in Lewis was renewed again. Before then, only serious students of art history were familiar with this pioneering artist.

That has changed today, thanks to new Lewis biographies and the discovery of her sculptures long thought to be lost. More than a century after her death, the artist is now the subject of *New York Times* articles again,[5] and a Google Doodle of her made its debut during Black History Month in 2017. That year also saw Edmonia

Google Doodle

The name "Edmonia Lewis" became familiar to the masses after Google chose her to be its "doodle" on February 1, 2017. Any Google users who visited the search engine on the first day of Black History Month that year saw an animated Lewis working on her *Death of Cleopatra* sculpture. Google Arts & Culture also provided a slideshow of Lewis's life and work, including sculptures such as 1856's *Puck*, 1872's *Poor Cupid*, and 1875's *Moses*. In addition, the presentation included a quote from Lewis about how she felt after arriving in Rome.

"I thought I knew everything when I came to Rome, but I soon found I had everything to learn," she said.[6]

By highlighting Lewis in this way, Google taught members of the public who had never heard of the artist all about her contributions to neoclassical sculpture.

Lewis's grave in St. Mary's Roman Catholic Cemetery in London get a marker after a fund-raising effort. For years, the site of her final resting place remained unknown, but scholars worked to track it down and give the artist the recognition she deserved. Now, her grave features a black marble marker with the following in gold letters: "Edmonia Lewis, Sculptor, 1844–1907."[7]

With no sculptors of color to turn to during her career, Edmonia Lewis is now a source of inspiration to artists and people of all backgrounds.

Chronology

1844

Edmonia Lewis is born in upstate New York.

1853

Edmonia becomes an orphan around this time.

1856

Edmonia attends New York Central College in McGrawville.

1859

John Brown's raid on Harpers Ferry ends in failure.
Edmonia Lewis enters Oberlin College.
John Brown is put to death.

1862

Lewis is accused of poisoning two Oberlin classmates.
Lawyer John Mercer Langston defends her and wins a not-guilty verdict.

1863

Lewis is accused of stealing art supplies from Oberlin.
She leaves Oberlin and heads to Boston.

1864

Lewis sculpts a bust of Colonel Robert Gould Shaw.

1865

Lewis leaves Boston for Florence, Italy.

1866

Lewis arrives in Rome.
The prestigious *Art Journal* runs an article about her.

1867

Lewis completes *Forever Free*, a sculpture celebrating slavery's end in America.

1870

Lewis returns to the United States.

1873

Lewis travels to the United States once more, taking the train to San Francisco.

1868

Henry Wadsworth Longfellow visits Rome, and Lewis completes a bust of him.

1870

Lewis meets the Third Marquess of Bute, who becomes a patron.

1876

Lewis brings *Death of Cleopatra* to the Centennial International Exposition in Philadelphia.
Actress Charlotte Cushman dies.

1877

Pope Pius IX visits Lewis's studio around this time.

1878

Lewis completes a bust of Ulysses S. Grant.

1879

Lewis travels to the United States and sells *The Veiled Bride of Spring*.

1889

Frederick Douglass and his wife visit Lewis in Rome.

1893

Lewis moves to Paris.

1901

Lewis moves to London.

1907

Lewis dies in Hammersmith, a section of West London. She identifies herself as "spinster and sculptor" in her will.

Chapter Notes

Chapter 1
A Connection with Frederick Douglass

1. Genevieve Ellerbee, "Voyage to Italia: Americans in Italy in the Nineteenth Century," Sheldon Museum of Art Catalogues and Publications, 2010, https://digitalcommons.unl.edu/cgi/viewcontent.cgi?article=1082&context=sheldonpubs.
2. Jone Johnson Lewis, "Helen Pitts Douglass," ThoughtCo.com, February 1, 2019, https://www.thoughtco.com/helen-pitts-douglass-biography-3530214.
3. Leigh Fought, *Women in the Life of Frederick Douglass* (New York, NY: Oxford University Press, 2017), p. 259.
4. Romare Bearden and Harry Henderson, *A History of African-American Artists: From 1792 to the Present* (New York, NY: Pantheon Books, 1993), p. 76.

Chapter 2
Edmonia's Early Years

1. Romare Bearden and Harry Henderson, *A History of African-American Artists: From 1792 to the Present* (New York: Pantheon Books, 1993), p. 54.
2. Bearden and Henderson, pp. 54–55.
3. Henry Wreford, "Lady Artists in Rome," *Art Journal*, March 1866, p. 177.
4. Bearden and Henderson, p. 56.
5. Mary Pickett, "Samuel W. Lewis: Orphan Leaves Mark on Bozeman," *Billings Gazette*, March 1, 2002, https://billingsgazette.com/lifestyles/samuel-w-lewis-orphan-leaves-mark-on-bozeman/article_bf7abce6-bbf5-5fe2-8269-d891f9e0682a.html.
6. Ibid.

7. Penelope Green, "Overlooked No More: Edmonia Lewis, Sculptor of Worldwide Acclaim," *New York Times*, July 25, 2018, https://www.nytimes.com/2018/07/25/obituaries/overlooked-edmonia-lewis-sculptor.html.
8. "Blacks and Whites Studied and Worked Together at Pre-Civil War College," Syracuse.com, February 3, 2012, https://www.syracuse.com/news/2012/02/new_york_central_college.html.
9. Ibid.

Chapter 3
The Trials of Oberlin

1. "John Brown's Raid on Harpers Ferry," History.com, February 27, 2019, https://www.history.com/this-day-in-history/john-browns-raid-on-harpers-ferry.
2. John Mercer Langston, *From the Virginia Plantation to the National Capitol: or, the First and Only Negro Representative in Congress from the Old Dominion* (Hartford, CT: American Publishing Company, 1894), pp. 173–174.
3. Langston, pp. 175–176.
4. Langston, p. 177.
5. "Langston, John Mercer (1829–1897)," Bioguide.Congress.gov, retrieved March 18, 2019, http://bioguide.congress.gov/scripts/biodisplay.pl?index=l000074.
6. Langston, pp. 179–180.

Chapter 4
Among the Abolitionists

1. Kevin Trimell Jones, "(Mary) Edmonia 'Wildfire' Lewis," Philadelphia Gay News, November 3, 2011, http://www.epgn.com/news/139-uncategorized/4011-16262425-mary-edmonia-wildfire-lewis-a-black-lesbian-who-sculpted-freedom-and-independence.

2. Romare Bearden and Harry Henderson, *A History of African-American Artists: From 1792 to the Present* (New York: Pantheon Books, 1993), pp. 58–59.

3. "Lydia Maria Child," Britannica.com, February 7, 2019, https://www.britannica.com/biography/Lydia-Maria-Child.

4. "A Chat with the Editor of the Standard," *The Liberator*, January 20, 1865, p. 12.

5. "A Chat with the Editor of the Standard," *The Liberator*, January 20, 1865, p. 12.

6. Ibid.

7. Ibid.

8. Ibid.

9. "Robert Gould Shaw," American Battlefield Trust, retrieved March 19, 2019, https://www.battlefields.org/learn/biographies/robert-gould-shaw.

Chapter 5
To the Eternal City

1. "A Chat with the Editor of the Standard," *The Liberator*, January 20, 1865, p. 12.

2. "The Greek Slave," National Gallery of Art, retrieved May 7, 2019, https://www.nga.gov/collection/art-object-page.166484.html.

3. "William Wetmore Story," Smithsonian American Art Museum, retrieved March 19, 2019, https://americanart.si.edu/artist/william-wetmore-story-4670.

4. Jeffrey Byrd, "Hosmer, Harriet Goodhue (1830–1908)," GLTBQArchive.com, 2015, http://www.glbtqarchive.com/arts/hosmer_h_A.pdf.

Chapter 6
A Shift in Focus

1. Henry Wreford, "Lady Artists in Rome," *Art Journal*, March 1866, p. 177
2. Ibid.
3. Ibid.
4. Ibid.
5. Kimberly Towne, "Making Art Against the Odds: The Triumph of Edmonia Lewis," retrieved March 20, 2019, https://teachers.yale.edu/curriculum/viewer/initiative_14.01.10_u.
6. Anne Whitney Papers, Wellesley College Archives, October 28, 1867.
7. "The Studios of Rome," *Art Journal*, 1870, p. 77.
8. Eric Hanks, "Rare Edmonia Lewis Photo Discovered," *International Review of African American Art*, retrieved March 20, 2019, http://iraaa.museum.hamptonu.edu/page/Rare-Edmonia-Lewis-Photo-Discovered.

Chapter 7
Longfellow and Hiawatha

1. Henry Tuckerman, *Book of the Artists: Comprising Biographical and Critical Sketches of the American Artists* (New York: G.P. Putnam's Sons, 1867), p. 604.
2. Ibid.
3. Tuckerman, p. 603.
4. *New York Times*, July 8, 1869, p. 5.

Chapter 8
Trips Back Home

1. Anne Whitney Papers, Wellesley College Archives, October 28, 1867.

2. "Black History Month: Edmonia Lewis," MountStuart. com, October 4, 2017, https://www.mountstuart.com/ black-history-month-edmonia-lewis/.

3. Ibid.

4. "Central Pacific Railroad," Britannica.com, February 15, 2019, https://www.britannica.com/topic/Central-Pacific-Railroad#ref112701.

Chapter 9
Cleopatra

1. Stephen May, "The Object at Hand," *Smithsonian Magazine*, September 1996, https://www.smithsonianmag.com/arts-culture/the-object-at-hand-4-121205387/.

2. *New York Herald*, July 11, 1876, p. 4.

3. Ibid.

4. *The Daily Graphic*, July 21, 1876, p. 2.

5. "Grant's World Tour," PBS.org, retrieved March 21, 2019, https://www.pbs.org/wgbh/americanexperience/features/grant-tour/.

Chapter 10
Lewis's Legacy

1. "Phillis Wheatley," PBS.org, retrieved March 22, 2019, https://www.pbs.org/wgbh/aia/part2/2p12.html.

2. Ibid.

3. "Biography - Chronology. Outline of Mary Edmonia Lewis's Life and Art," EdmoniaLewis.com, January 27, 2019, http://www.edmonialewis.com/chronology.htm.

4. Talia Lavin, "The Life and Death of Edmonia Lewis, Spinster and Sculptor," The Toast, November 2, 2015, http://the-toast.net/2015/11/02/the-life-and-death-of-edmonia-lewis/.

5. Penelope Green, "Overlooked No More: Edmonia Lewis, Sculptor of Worldwide Acclaim," *New York Times*, July 25, 2018, https://www.nytimes.com/2018/07/25/obituaries/overlooked-edmonia-lewis-sculptor.html.

6. "A Selection of Edmonia Lewis' Most Iconic Sculptures," Google Arts & Culture, February 1, 2017, https://artsandculture.google.com/exhibit/gQJi3NKm3VagLg.

7. Talia Lavin, "The Decades-Long Quest to Find and Honor Edmonia Lewis's Grave," Hyperallergic.com, March 28, 2018, https://hyperallergic.com/434881/edmonia-lewis-grave/.

Glossary

abolitionist A person who worked to end slavery.

bias Unfair treatment; showing favoritism for one group or subject and against another group or subject.

commission To hire someone to create a work or provide a service.

exonerate To clear of wrongdoing; acquit.

expatriate Person who has left their home country to live in another country.

freedmen The African Americans who received their freedom after being enslaved.

idyllic Calm and peaceful; heavenly.

indigenous Describes a person, group, animal, plant, etc. that is local to a certain place or region.

miscegenation The mixing of people from two different racial groups, either by marriage or sexual relations.

neoclassicism An art movement or style known for drawing inspiration from works of the past, especially ancient or classical art.

privileged Having wealth, power, or advantages that most people don't have.

progressive Open-minded or liberal.

ravage To damage or destroy.

stereotype A widespread idea or generalization about a group of people, often based on their race, gender, religion, nationality, or sexual orientation.

suffragist A person who works for the right to vote, especially for women.

Further Reading

BOOKS

Atkins, Jeannine. *Stone Mirrors: The Sculpture and Silence of Edmonia Lewis*. New York, NY: Atheneum Books, 2017.

Ingram, J. S. *The Centennial Exposition*. Philadelphia, PA: Hubbard Brothers, 1876.

O'Connor, Thomas H. *Civil War Boston: Home Front & Battlefield*. Boston, MA: Northeastern University Press, 1997.

Quinn, Bridget. *Broad Strokes: 15 Women Who Made Art and Made History (in That Order)*. San Francisco, CA: Chronicle Books, 2017.

Wolfe, Rinna Evelyn. *Edmonia Lewis: Wildfire in Marble*. Parsippany, NJ: Dillon Press, 1998.

WEBSITES

The Metropolitan Museum of Art
www.metmuseum.org/art/collection/search/687670
A webpage about Edmonia Lewis's *The Marriage of Hiawatha* as well as links to her other sculptures and related works of art.

The Smithsonian American Art Museum
americanart.si.edu/artist/edmonia-lewis-2914
The museum's webpage on Edmonia Lewis's art and life; it includes links to relevant exhibitions as well.

Index

Charlotte
Etinde-Crompton

Samuel
Willard Crompton

About the Authors

Charlotte Etinde-Crompton was born and raised in Zaire and came to Massachusetts at the age of twenty. Her artistic sensibility stems from her early exposure to the many talented artists of her family and tribe, which include master woodcarvers. She developed an interest in African American art after arriving in the United States.

Samuel Willard Crompton is a tenth-generation New Englander who now lives in metropolitan Atlanta. He was a history professor at Holyoke Community College for twenty-eight years. His interest in the arts comes from his wood-carving father and his oil-painting mother. Crompton is the author and editor of many books, including a number of nonfiction young adult titles with Enslow Publishing.